This edition copyright © 2002 Lion Publishing
Text copyright © 2002 Jean Watson

Published by
Lion Publishing plc
Mayfield House, 256 Banbury Road,
Oxford OX2 7DH, England
www.lion-publishing.co.uk
ISBN 0 7459 4656 9

First edition 2002
10 9 8 7 6 5 4 3 2 1 0

Acknowledgments

25, 30: Genesis 1:31; 1 Timothy 6:17, from the *Holy Bible, New International Version*, copyright © 1973, 1978, 1984 by International Bible Society. Used by permission.

Every effort has been made to trace and acknowledge copyright holders of all the quotations in this book. We apologize for any errors or omissions that may remain, and would ask those concerned to contact the publishers, who will ensure that full acknowledgment is made in the future.

A catalogue record for this book is available
from the British Library

Typeset in 12/14 Venetian 301
Printed and bound in China

beauty

new ways of seeing

Jean Watson

LION
GHlines

Contents

· · · · · · · · · · · · · · · · · · · ·

Introduction

. . . .

'Why bother with beauty? It's nice, but it's not exactly necessary, is it? We have to get on with the serious business of living — working to provide for ourselves and our families. There's no time for beauty.'

But in a world that holds so much pain and suffering as well as joy, it would seem a good idea to make the most of beauty in all its forms; to relish lovely people and every good moment, event, encounter. Purely at a pragmatic level this attitude is positive and attractive. And if, moreover, we view life as a gift to be cherished, it is not just advisable but right: a way of hearing through every good and beautiful thing 'echoes of mercy, whispers of love'; of affirming the ultimate truth about life and the universe; of celebrating the real hope and joy that keep breaking through even in our present shadowlands.

Open to beauty

A famous musician once said something like this: 'Music is in the air. You have only to listen to it.' The same thing applies to beauty. Beauty is all around us. We have only to be receptive to it.

When I think about my own receptivity to beauty – or lack of it – and what lies behind that, I realise that attitude and time are relevant and linked considerations. If we live life at a cracking pace, we will rush past beautiful things and people without a second glance. Do we have to live like this? Or are we afraid to slow down and reflect in any depth about what is really going on? Making space for beauty is difficult, but it can bring welcome relief and healing as well as opening us up to enjoy new aspects and depths of beauty, whether in nature's display of sensuous satisfactions or in the varieties of human loveliness and creativity.

Why not, today, stop when you see or hear something beautiful and just focus on enjoying it wholeheartedly?

Mary was at the window in a moment, and in a moment more it was opened wide and freshness and softness and scents and birds' songs were pouring through. 'That's fresh air,' she said. 'Lie on your back and draw in long breaths of it.'

Frances Hodgson Burnett

The tree which moves some to tears of joy is in the eyes of others only a green thing which stands in the way. As a man is, so he sees.

William Blake

Beauty in things exists in the mind which contemplates them.

David Hume

We are born and placed among
wonders and surrounded by them,
so that to whatever object the eye
first turns, the same is wonderful
and full of wonders, if only we
would examine it for a while.

John de Dondis

The eyes are blind:
one must look with the heart.

Antoine de Saint-Exupéry

In spite of all,
Some shape of beauty
   moves away the pall
From our dark spirits.

John Keats

Too late came I to love thee, O thou
Beauty both so ancient and so fresh.

St Augustine of Hippo

Flowers have an expression of
countenance as much as men or
animals. Some seem to smile, some
are pensive and diffident, others
again are plain, honest and upright
like the broad-faced sunflower and
the hollyhock.

Henry Ward Beecher

The mountains are God's
   majestic thoughts.
The stars are God's
   brilliant thoughts.
The flowers are God's
   beautiful thoughts.

Robert Stuart MacArthur

Beauty is God's handwriting.

Charles Kingsley

What you are seeking may be found
in a single rose or a drop of water.

Antoine de Saint-Exupéry

In all ranks of life the human heart
yearns for the beautiful; and the
beautiful things that God makes
are his gifts to all alike.

Harriet Beecher Stowe

The gift of beauty

Reading through a
list of flower names
is almost like reading
poetry. The words are
so beautiful. Amaryllis,
daffodil, snowdrop,
clematis; peony, anemone,
hosta, iris; crucifer, gillyflower, aster, daisy;
edelweiss, kalmia, azalea, lily; agapanthus,
crocus, celandine; hyacinth, zinnia, columbine.
And these flowers are beautiful in colour and
shape, scent and texture as well as in name.

But beauty can be dangerous. Monkshood
is tall and elegant, with dark green glossy
leaves and flowers of different shades of blue
or white, off-white or delicate pink. But it is
very poisonous.

What are we to do with beauty? Obviously, if it is in any way harmful, we need to reject it. But otherwise we should treat it like the precious gift it is. In Greek legend Narcissus, rejected by Echo, fell in love with his own reflection in the water and was changed into a flower as a punishment for his vanity. To worship beauty – whether one's own or anyone else's – is to abuse the gift and slight the giver. To enjoy it, use it thoughtfully, wisely and well and share it generously is to reap its full benefit.

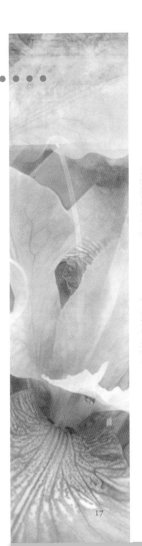

It is amazing how complete is the
delusion that beauty is goodness.

Leo Tolstoy

Beauty without virtue is a flower
without perfume.

French saying

Enter these enchanted wood,
You who dare.
Nothing harms beneath the leaves,
More than waves a swimmer cleaves.
Toss your heart up with the lark,
Foot at peace with mouse and worm,
Fare you fair.

George Meredith

Give beauty back, beauty, beauty,
beauty back to God,
beauty's self and beauty's giver.

Gerard Manley Hopkins

All of creation God gives
to humankind to use.

Hildegard of Bingen

This we know: the earth
does not belong to man;
man belongs to the earth.
Whatever befalls the earth
befalls the sons of the earth.
Man did not weave the web
of life; he is merely a strand
in it. Whatever he does to
the web, he does to himself.

Indian tribal leader

Nature is painting for us, day
after day, pictures of infinite beauty,
if only we have eyes to see them.

John Ruskin

Everything has life, in a spiritual
conception, and everything carries
an element of divine beauty in its
being. It is for us to discover and
reveal it, either in poetry or prose,
in art or sculpture, in work or play.

Alison Uttley

Art supposes that beauty is not
an exception, but is the basis for
an order. The transcendental face
of art is always a form of prayer.

John Berger

• •

Never lose an opportunity of seeing anything that is beautiful; for beauty is God's handwriting – a wayside sacrament. Welcome it in every fair face, in every fair sky, in every fair flower, and thank God for it as a cup of blessing.

Ralph Waldo Emerson

When I am working on a problem, I never think about beauty. I think only how to solve the problem. But when I have finished, if the solution is not beautiful, I know it is wrong.

Buckminster Fuller

I have loved the principle of beauty in all things.

John Keats

True beauty

● ● ● ● ● ● ● ● ● ● ● ●

I don't know how you would define beauty.
Recently I flicked through a magazine at the
hairdresser's and came across pages and pages
of photographs of 'the most beautiful women
in the world'. Certainly they were physically
very lovely. For all I know, they could have
had lovely characters as well.

There's a song that goes, 'Keep young and
beautiful, if you want to be loved.' I grew up
thinking I was certainly plain and probably
ugly, and either way handsome princes were
way out of my reach. I am sure a great many
people feel this way as they see media images
of physical beauty and desirability – of which
they fall far short.

We may need to hear many alternative
messages and be given much genuine love and
affirmation before we feel able to hold up our
heads with everyone else. For the truth is that
you do *not* have to keep young and beautiful,

as defined by the media, in order to be loved.
True love sees the loved person as beautiful
in ways that matter to him or her – and
transitory conditions such as youth and
'beauty' are neither here nor there.

Would it be good to tell someone you love
that he or she is special and lovely to you?

The story tells us that the ugly duckling never was a duckling. He was always a swan. Each of us is a swan, for this is the nature of man, a spiritual being and infinitely desirable. For here beauty is a symbol of desirability. All the others were wrong, blind to his true potential.

Pat Wynnejones

The human face is the masterpiece of God. The eyes reveal the soul, the mouth the flesh. The chin stands for purpose, the nose means will. But over and behind all is that fleeting something we call 'expression'.

Elbert Hubbard

Oh, happy eyes,
Whatever you have seen,
Let it be as it may be,
It has been so beautiful.

Johann Wilhelm von Goethe

What makes an object beautiful is
a combination of order and disorder:
the fact that the simple geometry of
the perfect shape is subtly disrupted.
The oak leaf is not quite symmetrical;
each larch tree I can see, in its fight
for light and air, has ended up with its
left side a little different from its right;
the tips of each lupin leaf do not quite
form a perfect circle.

Michael Mayne

God saw all that he had made,
and it was very good.

The Bible

With happy people
I always found, deep down,
a sense of security,
a great simplicity,
and a spontaneous joy
in little things.

Philip Bosmans

If ever any beauty I did see,
Which I desired and got,
'Twas but a dream of thee.

John Donne

Is she kind as she is fair?
For beauty lives with kindness.

William Shakespeare

'I'd like you to meet the woman who changed my life,' he said. His face was very solemn, but Lucy was smiling. 'Your what?' she seemed to be saying. 'Your, what was that? Oh, your *life*.' And she tipped her head and smiled. After all, she might have said, this was an ordinary occurrence. People changed other people's lives every day of the year. There was no call to make such a fuss about it

Anne Tyler

I think true love is never blind,
But rather brings an added light,
An inner vision quick to find
The beauties hid from common sight.

Phoebe Cary

• • • • • • • • • •

Special places

At the top of my garden is a secluded, steeply banked wooded place. It was while standing there that my late husband and I decided to buy the house where I still live. This was always a special place for him and he especially loved the enormous cherry tree right on the boundary of our land which produced a mass of deep pink blossom every year. Our children loved the place too – they climbed the trees there and swung on a tyre attached to an overhanging branch. Now he is gone and they are grown and the tree was felled in a hurricane. But I have lovely memories – and dream of making something of this beautiful place once again if I possibly can.

Beautiful places can be anywhere. At the bottom of the garden where there might be fairies! A holiday place which proved to be the best ever. Bed is a beautiful place for weary people or lovers.

Home for many is the
most beautiful place in
the world.

Are you making the
most of your special
places?

God richly provides us with everything
for our enjoyment.

The Bible

I remember a house where all were good
To me, God knows, deserving no such thing:
Comforting smell breathed at very entering,
Fetched fresh, as I suppose, off some sweet
wood.

Gerard Manley Hopkins

The beauty of a house is harmony.

Frank Crane

There is beauty all around
When there's love at home.

Author unknown

'Tis the sense
Of majesty and beauty and repose,
A blended holiness of earth and sky,
Something that makes this individual spot,
This small abiding-place of many men,
A whole without dependence or defect,
Made for itself and happy in itself,
Perfect contentment, unity entire.

William Wordsworth

When I was quite a boy, my father used to take me to the Montpelier Tea-gardens at Walworth. I unlock the casket of memory and see the beds of larkspur with purple eyes; tall holy-oaks, red and yellow; the broad sunflowers, caked in gold with bees buzzing round them.

William Hazlitt

Nothing is more beautiful than the loveliness of woods before sunrise.

George Washington Carver

Surely that breeze that o'er the blue wave curled
Did whisper soft, 'Thy wanderings here are
    blessed.'
How different from the language of the world!
Nor jeers nor taunts in this still spot are given:
Its calm's a balsam to a soul distressed;
And, where peace smiles, a wilderness is heaven.

John Clare

The little cares that fretted me,
I lost them yesterday,
Among the fields above the sea,
Among the winds at play,
Among the lowing of the herds,
The rustling of the trees,
Among the singing of the birds,
The humming of the bees.

Elizabeth Barrett Browning

Beautiful experiences

Just keeping our eyes and ears open brings us a whole host of beautiful experiences. For a few short weeks, I can drink in the pale pink and white beauty of a sprawling magnolia tree in the garden next door or, on my walk to the post box, stop to admire a stylish camellia with its dark green glossy leaves and wide-open deep pink flowers.

I began compiling a list of beautiful experiences to be encountered just within the boundaries of ordinary everyday life and experience. Here are a few of them…

The dawn chorus, or just listening to a lovely speaking voice. Waking up with something to look forward to, or with no headache after days of migraine. An invitation from a friend; thoughtful, kind cards, visits, letters, phone calls, e-mails. An appreciative comment; a shared joke; a pleasant surprise. A child's wide-eyed wonder and artless, unaffected delight; a baby's chuckle.

A cool drink on a hot day; a cup of tea. A bath; a fire on a cold evening. The aroma of fresh coffee, warm bread or new-mown grass. A daisy. The sounds created by a thunderstorm, or the softer music of a playful breeze or a running stream. Silence. Trees, clouds, dappled sunlight, a rainbow. The night sky… There are so many wonders to be enjoyed. Take a walk and discover some of them as soon as possible!

Even a walk to the mailbox
is a precious experience.

John Updike

A walk: the air incredibly pure, delights
for the eye, a warm and gently caressing
sunlight, one's whole being joyous.

Henri Frédéric Amiel

A flower has opened in my heart…
It is the peace that shines apart,
The peace of daybreak skies that bring
Clear song and wild swift wing.

Siegfried Sassoon

The sight of a magnificent sunset was sometimes almost more than I could endure and made me wish to hide myself away. But when the feeling was roused by the sight of a small and beautiful or singular object, such as a flower, its sole effect was to intensify the object's loveliness.

W.H. Hudson

How sweet the moonlight sleeps
upon this bank!

William Shakespeare

Look at the stars! Look, look up at the skies!
O look at all the fire-folk sitting in the air!

Gerard Manley Hopkins

● ● ● ● ● ● ● ●

In sweet music is such art,
Killing care and grief of heart.

William Shakespeare

Music, the greatest good that
    mortals know,
And all of heaven we have below.

Joseph Addison

Music, when soft voices die,
Vibrates in the memory.

Percy Bysshe Shelley

Every sound is sweet;
Myriads of rivulets hurrying through the lawn,
The moan of doves in immemorial elms,
And murmuring of innumerable bees.
There's music in the sighing of a reed;
There's music in the gushing of a rill;
There's music in all things, if men had ears;
The earth is but the music of the spheres.

Lord Byron

If you get simple beauty and naught else,
You get about the best thing God invents.

Robert Browning

Changes and choices

I remember as a young person
giving a recording of a musical
I absolutely loved to a favourite
aunt and uncle. I so much wanted
to give them the enjoyment I had
received from the story and the
songs. They thanked me politely,
but it was obvious that the
musical had not done for them
what it had done for me!
Perhaps, had they been my age,
it might have. Or perhaps at any
age their musical and dramatic
tastes were different from mine.

It's certainly true that our
idea of what's delightful and
beautiful changes at different
stages in our lives. A six-year-old's
idea of heaven on earth might
be fun, presents and chocolate;
a ninety-six-year-old's, a quiet

life, a clear conscience and happy memories.

But some things don't change. Love, the real thing, is beautiful at any age. And I want always to keep in touch with and give rein to certain aspects of childlikeness in me. Wonder, joy, trust, a willingness to experiment and discover, to absorb, have fun, enjoy and learn.

Thinking of your attitude to and your awareness and appreciation of beauty, what has changed and what has endured over the years?

In childhood we discover the world afresh. Nothing is banal, every stick and stone carries a breath of life.

Alison Uttley

Trees have the power to startle me more and more.

Philip Toynbee

Most people simply don't know how beautiful the world is and how much splendour is revealed in the smallest things, in a common flower, in a stone, in the bark of a tree or the leaf of a birch. Grown-up people gradually lose the eye for these riches which children quickly notice and love with their whole heart.

Rainer Maria Rilke

Ageing calls us into the lowly
simplicities that we thought
we had outgrown as children.

John Updike

I have learned
To look on nature,
    not as in the hour
Of thoughtless youth;
    but hearing oftentimes
The still, sad music of humanity.

William Wordsworth

Familiarity with nature never
breeds contempt. The more
one learns, the more he expects
surprises, and the more he
becomes aware of the inscrutable.

Archibald Rutledge

Anyone who keeps the ability to see beauty never grows old.

Franz Kafka

Happily, there exists more than one kind of beauty. There is the beauty of infancy, the beauty of youth, the beauty of maturity and the beauty of age.

George Augustus Sala

A thing of beauty is a joy for ever;
Its loveliness increases; it will never
Pass into nothingness;

but still will keep
A bower quiet for us,
and a sleep
Full of sweet dreams
and health and
quiet breathing.

John Keats

The longer I live, the more my mind
dwells upon the beauty and wonder
of the world. I have loved the feel
of the grass under my feet, and the
sound of the running streams by my
side. The hum of the winds in the
treetops has always been good music
to me, and the face of the fields has
often comforted me more than the
faces of men.

John Burroughs

I have been here before,
But when or how I cannot tell:
I know the grass beyond the door,
The sweet keen smell,
The sighing sound,
The lights around the shore.

Dante Gabriel Rossetti